DISCOVERY SCIENCE

WEATHER

KINGFISHER

First published in 2012 by Kingfisher
This edition published 2017 by Kingfisher
an imprint of Macmillan Children's Books
20 New Wharf Road, London N1 9RR
Associated companies throughout the world
www.panmacmillan.com

ISBN 978-0-7534-4146-6

First published as *Kingfisher Young Knowledge: Weather* in 2006
Additional material produced for Macmillan Children's Books by Discovery Books Ltd
Cover design: Wildpixel Ltd

Copyright © Macmillan Publishers International Ltd 2012

9 8 7 6 5 4 3 2 1
1TR/0517/UTD/WKT/128MA

A CIP catalogue record for this book is available from the British Library.

Printed in China

Note to readers: the website addresses listed in this book are correct at the time of going to print.
However, due to the ever-changing nature of the internet, website addresses and content can
change. Websites can contain links that are unsuitable for children. The publisher cannot be held
responsible for changes in website addresses or content, or for information obtained through
a third party. We strongly advise that internet searches be supervised by an adult.

Acknowledgements
The publisher would like to thank the following for permission to reproduce their material.
b = bottom, *c* = centre, *l* = left, *t* = top, *r* = right

Photographs: Cover iStock; 1 iStock; 2–3 iStock/valdezri; 4–5 Getty/Erik Buraas; 6tr Alamy/Travelshots;
6bl Getty/Christopher Furlong; 7 Corbis/ Don Mason; 8 Getty/Manoj Shah; 9tl Corbis/Nevada Weir;
9r Superstock/Raith/Mauritus; 10–11 Alamy/Richard Cooke; 11tl Science Photo Library (SPL)/Simon Fraser;
12–13 Getty/Emmanuel Faure; 12cr Getty/Johannes Caspersen; 14–15 Getty/Fritz Poelking; 15tl iStock/Jacques van
Dinteren; 15cr Alamy/Mike Greenslade; 16–17 Corbis/Roy Morsch; 16 iStock/4nadia; 18–19 Shutterstock/Minerva
Studio; 18b Corbis/Remi Benali; 19tr Shutterstock/phofotos; 20–21 Getty/David Tipling; 21 Getty/Stockbyte;
22 iStock/onzeg; 23 Getty/Tom Brakefield; 23tr SPL/Pekka Parviainen; 24–25 iStock/PeopleImages; 25tl Getty/Marc
Muench; 25br Getty/Jami Tarris; 26 Getty/Gandee Vasan; 27tl Corbis/Jim Reed; 27 iStock/switas;
28–29 iStock/Africanway; 29tl iStpck/gdagys; 29br Getty/Turner Forte; 30–31 Getty/Rosemary Calvert;
30l iStock/AlesValuscek; 31 Getty/Andre Gallant; 32–33 iStock/Nataliiap; 32t Getty/David Hiser; 32b Getty/Gerbern
Oppermans; 34–35 Getty/David Olsen; 35 Alamy/Steve Bloom; 36–37 Getty/Per-Anders Pettersson; 36cr Getty/David
McNew; 37br Getty/Doug Menuez; 38–39 Getty/Nick Caloyianis; 38bl Masterfile; 38br Corbis/Jim Reed; 40 Keren Su
Corbis; 41tl iStock/Bernhard Staehli; 41br Alamy/Zute Lightfoot; 48 Shutterstock/nadiya_sergey; 49t Shutterstock/Yuriy
Poznuknov; 49b Shutterstock/Hector Conesa; 52tr Shutterstock Images/Yevgeniy11; 52bl Shutterstock/Jaroslav Bartos;
53 Shutterstock/Pakhnyushchy; 56 Shutterstock/Jokerpro

Commissioned photography on pages 42–47 by Andy Crawford
Thank you to models Dilvinder Dilan Bhamra, Cherelle Clarke, Madeleine Roffey and William Sartin

WEATHER

Caroline Harris

KINGFISHER

Contents

What is weather?

Weather is all the changes that happen in the air. Water, air and heat from the Sun work together to make weather.

Warm and sunny

When the Sun is high in the sky and there are not many clouds, the weather is hot and dry. If it is cloudy, the temperature will be lower.

Let the rain fall

Without water, there would be no life on the Earth. Rain helps plants to grow and gives animals water to drink.

Icy water

Water freezes when it is very cold. This changes the weather. Snow falls instead of rain, and water on the ground turns to ice.

Our star

The Sun is a burning hot star. It is so bright, it lights up the Earth. The Sun also helps to make our weather. It heats the land and air to make winds blow, and it warms oceans to make clouds and rain.

Night and day

The Earth spins around once every 24 hours. When one side of the Earth faces the Sun, it is daytime there. On the other side of Earth, it is night-time.

Sun worship

The Incas lived many years ago in South America. They worshipped the Sun. In those days, a lot of people thought the Sun was a god because it was so powerful.

Burning heat

The Sun's rays can easily burn people's skin. Stay safe in the Sun by covering up and using suncream. Never look straight at the Sun.

Blanket of air

The atmosphere is a layer of air that covers the Earth. It is where all weather happens. The atmosphere keeps our planet warm and protects it from danger, such as being hit by space rocks.

Blue skies
The sky looks blue on a clear day. This is because of the way sunlight shines through the Earth's atmosphere.

Breathe in

The atmosphere is made up of a mixture of gases. Both plants and animals need these gases to live.

Up and away

The atmosphere has five layers. The one closest to Earth is the troposphere. This is where clouds form. The layer furthest from Earth is the exosphere.

Layers of the atmosphere

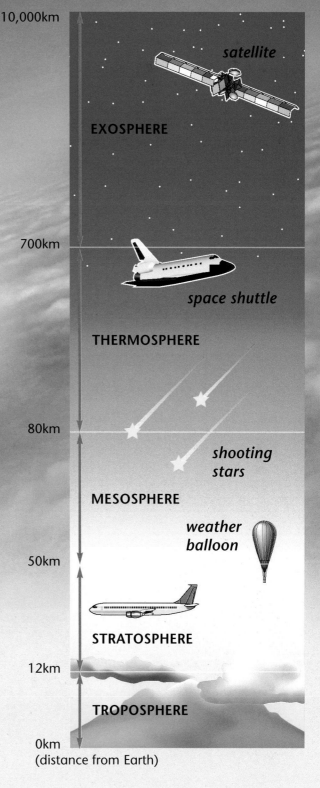

10,000km

satellite

EXOSPHERE

700km

space shuttle

THERMOSPHERE

80km

shooting stars

MESOSPHERE

weather balloon

50km

STRATOSPHERE

12km

TROPOSPHERE

0km
(distance from Earth)

Changing seasons

Most countries have four seasons: spring, summer, autumn and winter. Seasons change because of the way Earth orbits the Sun. Each orbit takes one year.

Earth on the move

The Earth tilts, so each pole is nearer the Sun and is warmer at different times of the year. When it is summer in the north, it is winter in the south.

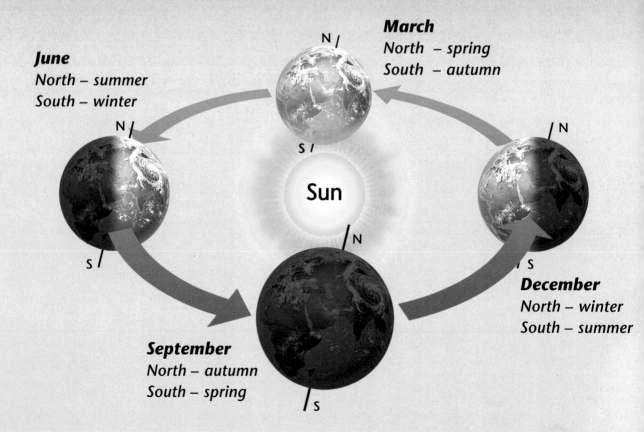

March
North – spring
South – autumn

June
North – summer
South – winter

Sun

December
North – winter
South – summer

September
North – autumn
South – spring

Spring and summer

In spring, flowers come out and many animals have babies. The warm weather of summer follows spring.

spring

Autumn and winter

At the end of summer, autumn arrives and the leaves fall off the trees. Then comes chilly winter.

autumn

World climates

The normal weather in a place is called its climate. There are different types of climate around the world. Some are hot and dry, while others are freezing cold, or warm and wet.

Icy cold

Antarctica has the coldest climate on Earth. The emperor penguins that live there have blubber and special feathers to help them stay warm.

Hot and dry

Deserts form where the climate is very dry and usually cloudless. They can change from sizzling hot during the day to freezing cold at night.

Warmed by the ocean

In Cornwall, UK, there are palm trees, which usually grow only in hotter places. A warm sea current makes the climate mild.

Blowing about

The air in the atmosphere is always on the move, blowing from one place to another. This is wind. Some winds are only gentle breezes. Gales are strong winds that blow tiles off roofs and people off their feet!

Weather vane
Whenever the wind blows a weather vane around, the arrow on it turns. The arrow stops once it points the way the wind is blowing from.

Flying kites
People have been flying
kites for thousands of years.
The wind lifts the kite, and
the owner can pull or steer
it with a long string.

Wild winds

Strong winds can be very dangerous. They knock down buildings and injure people. But they are also useful – wind turbines can make electricity.

Dust storm

In places where the soil is dry, strong winds can make huge clouds of dust. These dust storms move quickly and can blow grit into eyes, clothes and hair.

Twisting winds

A tornado is a spinning funnel of wind that comes from a storm cloud. Some tornadoes are so powerful that they can suck a house off the ground.

Whistling wind

The wind whistles when it blows hard through a small gap. It is the same as when someone whistles through their lips.

Blue planet

Water covers much of the Earth. As the Sun warms seas and lakes, it turns the water into vapour. This is in the air, but it cannot be seen.

The water cycle

Water is always moving. When it rains, water runs into rivers, which flow into the sea. From there, it turns into vapour and makes clouds. Then it rains again.

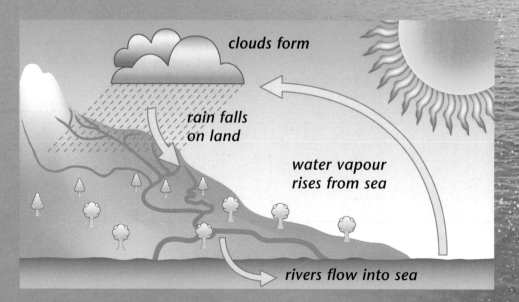

clouds form

rain falls on land

water vapour rises from sea

rivers flow into sea

Healthy water

Humans are also part of the water cycle. Mineral and tap water were once rain. People need to drink several glasses of water every day to stay healthy.

dolphins in the ocean

Enormous oceans

Oceans cover 72 per cent of the Earth's surface. They have a huge effect on our weather. Ocean currents carry with them warm, cold or wet weather.

Mist and clouds

Clouds can be made from tiny drops of water or from ice crystals. They are formed when warm air holding water vapour cools down. Clouds come in all shapes and sizes.

Fluffy cumulus

A cloud's name describes how high up it is and what it looks like. For example, the fluffy clouds seen in warm weather are called cumulus.

Glowing in the night

Some clouds glow in the dark, just after sunset. They look bright blue and are criss-crossed with wavy lines.

Tiger in the mist

Mist and fog are cloud near the ground. They usually form in cool weather. This tiger's home in the jungle is very wet, so it is misty there even though it is warm.

Out in the **rain**

A raindrop is made when tiny drops of water in a cloud touch and join together. The raindrop gets larger and heavier, and finally it falls to the ground as rain.

The shape of rain

Rain may look like lines, but each raindrop is usually the shape of a sphere. Most are small – the size of a pencil tip.

Carried by the wind

Storms produce enormous, heavy raindrops. Strong winds keep the rain up in the air for a long time, so the drops get really big.

Leafy umbrella

Like humans, many animals like to shelter from the rain. Orang-utans hold handfuls of leaves above their heads to stop getting wet.

Stormy days

A thunderstorm happens when clouds grow bigger and taller, and gather more and more energy. Every day, there can be as many as 40,000 storms crashing down around the world.

Lightning strikes

Lightning is a spark of electricity that makes the air glow. It can move between clouds or shoot down to the ground, onto trees or buildings.

High as a mountain

Thunderclouds can be enormous. In very severe storms, they can be taller than a mountain!

Hurricane damage

A hurricane is a group of thunderstorms that spin. At the centre is a calm circle called the eye. When a hurricane hits the land, it can cause a lot of damage.

Wet and dry

Some parts of the world are rainy and wet. Other places are very dry. In deserts, years may pass without rain. But in the jungle, it can rain heavily all year long.

Pumping water
During a drought, there is not much rain. In very dry areas, people may have to walk to a well to get drinking water.

Water everywhere

When a lot of rain falls, it can cause floods. These are lakes of water that can cover a large area, even a whole city.

Dry earth

When it does not rain for a long time, the earth can become so dry and hard that it cracks.

Big freeze

When water gets very cold, it freezes into solid, slippery ice. You can see this as frost on plants and lawns, or the frozen, hard layer on a pond.

Handful of ice
Hailstones are balls of ice made in the thunderclouds. They fall like rain and the largest ones can be the size of a grapefruit. Ouch!

Feathery crystals

Frost forms when air near the ground is wet and so cold that it freezes. When it is warmer, this wetness makes dew instead.

Mountains of ice

Ice weighs less than water. This is why huge icebergs float. But only a small part of the ice can be seen. The rest is hidden underwater.

Flakes of snow

Snowflakes are made from ice that forms high up in the clouds. In warm weather, the ice melts and falls to the ground as rain or sleet. If it is cold enough, it falls as snow.

Cosy snow

Snow can keep you warm! The Inuit people, who live in the Arctic, make buildings called igloos from blocks of snow.

Snow shapes

Most snow crystals have six sides, but they never look exactly the same as each other. They all form different, beautiful patterns.

Snowfall

Snowflakes are snow crystals that are stuck together. Big flakes form when it is just below freezing. This is when the crystals are stickiest.

Light shows

Sometimes, water and ice crystals can make light look very colourful or unusual. They can cause amazing effects, such as sun dogs and the beautiful glowing light of a rainbow.

Colourful rainbow

When it rains and is sunny at the same time, it is sometimes possible to see a rainbow. This is especially clear if a dark cloud lies behind the rain.

Sun dogs

The two lights either side of the Sun are called sun dogs. They happen when sunlight shines through ice crystals in a particular way. The lights follow the Sun like a dog follows its owner.

Extreme weather

Sometimes the weather can be wild and dangerous. Extreme weather can cause storms, floods, wildfires and droughts.

Water power

Floods may stretch over huge distances and cause a lot of damage. They can leave people stranded, so that they need to be rescued by helicopter or by boat.

Fighting fire

Wildfires break out in hot weather. This is because trees and plants dry out, and then burn easily.

El Niño

This is a current of warm
water in the Pacific Ocean
that happens every few years.
It can cause terrible floods,
droughts and storms.

Rain or shine?

Weather forecasts tell us what the weather will be like for the next few days. Scientists use instruments and computers to make these forecasts.

Storm spotting

Trucks fitted with radar can find storms that are far away. Scientists then follow the storms and measure their strength.

Damp seaweed

There are easy ways of forecasting weather. For example, seaweed gets fat and floppy in wet air. This might mean that rain is coming.

Weather balloons
Scientists use balloons
to lift instruments high
into the sky. These then
measure the weather.

Future weather

The Earth's climate naturally goes through times when it is a lot warmer or icier than it is today. However, many scientists believe that humans are changing the weather.

Smokey cars

The weather may be changing because of pollution. It traps too much of the Sun's heat. This heat would normally escape into space.

Getting warmer

Earth's climate is heating up. This makes ice melt and break away from icebergs and glaciers. As a result, the levels of the oceans rise and flood areas of land.

Help for farmers

Scientists are now better at forecasting weather several months ahead. Farmers use these forecasts to help them decide which crops to plant each year.

Riding the wind

Making a kite

Kites soar in the sky because the wind pushes them upwards. Decorate yours with an animal face – try a tiger!

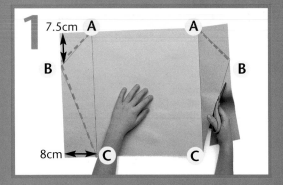

Following the measurements shown above, draw lines between A and C, A and B and B and C. Cut the paper from C to B and B to A.

You will need

- Sheet of A3 paper
- Ruler
- Pencil
- Scissors
- Felt-tip pens
- Sticky tape
- Hole punch
- 2 long drinking straws
- Coloured tissue paper
- Thin cotton string
- Thin stick

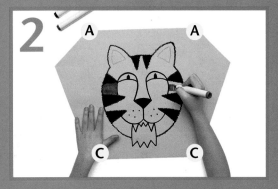

Turn the paper over and decorate your kite. You could draw a tiger. Make sure A is at the top of the kite and C is at the bottom.

Put sticky tape on the corners of the paper at B. Then use the hole punch to make holes through the tape 2.5cm from the edge, at B.

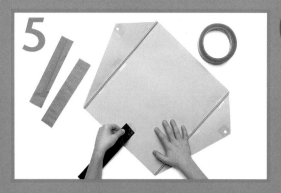

Turn the kite over. Use the sticky tape to fasten the straws on both sides of the paper along the line between A and C.

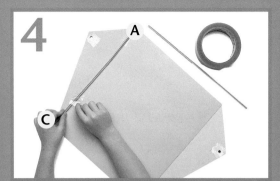

Using the scissors, cut strips of coloured tissue paper 20cm long. Stick the strips along the bottom edge of the kite.

Now your kite is ready to fly! Take a trip to the park and ask an adult to throw the kite high into the air. Pull it along, holding tightly onto the stick.

Thread 80cm of string through the punched-out holes and tie the ends together. The sides of the kite should bend inwards slightly. Wind another, long piece of string onto the stick. Tie the end to the middle of the string on the kite.

Sun dancer

Flashing lights

Your sun dancer will sparkle in the sunlight. If you place it near fruit bushes, it can help to scare away birds and stop them eating berries.

1 Place two CDs on paper with the shiny side facing down. Spread on glue. Stick the CDs together. Leave to dry. Repeat with the other CDs.

You will need
- 6 blank CDs
- Glue for plastic/paper
- Shiny cardboard
- Pencil
- Scissors
- Thread (6 x 20cm, 2 x 25cm, 1 x 35cm)
- String (35cm)
- Small bells
- Stick (25cm)

2 Draw six moons and six stars on cardboard. Cut them out. Stick two star shapes together, shiny side out. Repeat with all shapes.

3 Ask an adult to make a small hole in the point of each star and moon. Poke 20cm of thread into each hole and pull it halfway through.

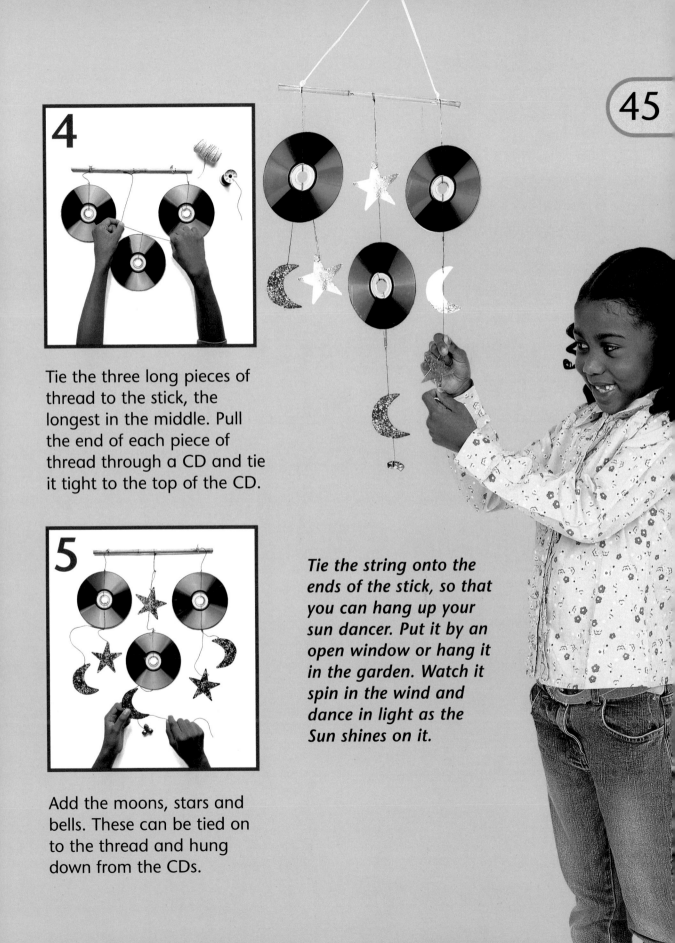

4

Tie the three long pieces of thread to the stick, the longest in the middle. Pull the end of each piece of thread through a CD and tie it tight to the top of the CD.

5

Add the moons, stars and bells. These can be tied on to the thread and hung down from the CDs.

Tie the string onto the ends of the stick, so that you can hang up your sun dancer. Put it by an open window or hang it in the garden. Watch it spin in the wind and dance in light as the Sun shines on it.

Creating colours

Make a rainbow

See how water is able to split light into different colours to make an amazing rainbow in your home.

You will need
- Glass jar
- Small mirror
- Torch
- Water jug

1

Place the glass jar on a table in a room with plain, light walls. Use the jug to half fill the jar with warm water.

2

Put the mirror in the jar and tilt it slightly upwards. Draw the curtains and turn out the lights so the room is very dark.

rainbow

Shine the torch on to the mirror and a rainbow should appear on the wall.

Swirling winds

Make a tornado

The swirling water in this experiment acts in the same way as the spinning winds of a wild tornado.

You will need
- Big, plastic bottle with cap
- Washing-up liquid
- Food colouring
- Glitter

Fill the bottle with water and add three drops of washing-up liquid and some food colouring. Shake in some glitter, which will act like the dust that a tornado picks up.

tornado

Screw the cap back on tightly, then swirl your bottle around in circles. Put it down quickly and watch what happens.

Glossary

Arctic – the area around the North Pole

Blubber – a layer of fat

Breeze – a gentle, light wind

Crystal – a substance or mineral found in nature, which has formed into a regular shape

Current – a river of warmer or cooler water in the ocean

Cycle – events that happen again and again in the same order

Dew – drops of water that form on grass and other surfaces when vapour in the air cools

Drought – a long period without rain

Effects – the results

Energy – power and force

Extreme – most unusual or severe

Fog – a thick cloud of tiny water droplets in the atmosphere

Freeze – to turn to ice

Frost – small, white ice crystals that form on the ground when the temperature falls below freezing

Funnel – a tube shape with a wider top and narrower bottom

Gases – shapeless substances, such as air, that are not solid or liquid

Glacier – a solid river of ice

Instruments – tools used to take measurements

Jungle – a hot, wet place full of trees and plants

Mineral water – water found in nature, often bottled and sold as drinking water

Ocean – a very large area of sea

Orbit – to move in a complete circle around a star or planet

Pole – the point furthest north or furthest south on a planet

Pollution – harmful dirt, such as exhaust fumes from cars

Produce – to make

Radar – an instrument that can locate objects far away by bouncing sounds off them

Sphere – a ball shape

Star – a large ball of burning gas in space, which appears as a point of light in the night sky

Temperature – how hot or cold it is

Vapour – tiny drops of water in the air, which look like mist

Well – a deep hole that leads to water under the ground

Wildfire – a fire in forest or grassland

Wind turbine – a machine that turns in the wind to make electricity

Worship – to show something love or respect by praying, chanting or singing

Ray – a beam of light that travels in a straight line

Severe – strong and powerful

Shelter – to protect from bad weather or danger

Sleet – rain mixed with snow or hail

Solid – not a liquid or a gas

This book includes material that would be particularly useful in helping to teach children aged 7–11. It covers many elements of the English and Science curricula and provides opportunities for cross-curricular lessons, especially those involving Geography and Art.

Extension activities

Writing
Find all the animals in this book and write an illustrated report describing how they deal with different kinds of weather.

Write a poem about the rain, describing how it feels and looks. Page 24 has information about rain.

Imagine you are a drop of water. Write a diary or story showing how you travel through the water cycle. The water cycle is explained on page 20.

Write a story where the characters are affected by extreme weather.

Examples of extreme weather are given on pages 36–37.

Read pages 40–41 about future weather. Write a one- or two-page report with ideas about what we can do to stop the climate changing.

Speaking and listening
Look at page 11. Imagine you are a reporter travelling in a balloon up through the atmosphere, and make a 'live' radio report about what you see.

Prepare a weather forecast and present it to a group of friends. Make it as interesting as you can!

Science
This book contains background on solids and liquids (pp7, 22–23, 30–31, 32–33), Earth and beyond (pp8, 10–11, 12–13, 40–41) and habitats (pp14–15, 21, 28, 33).

Cross-curricular links
The whole book links with the geography topics of weather and water.

Art: Look at pages 12–13. Create a collage of the seasons. Make sure you use different colours to show different seasons.

Look at page 33. Can you make a paper snowflake? Cut out a circle of tissue paper. Fold it in half and then into three so you have a thick wedge. Cut out shapes and open it up to reveal your snowflake.

Using the projects

Children can follow or adapt these projects at home. Here are some ideas for extending them:

Pages 42–43: Can you change your kite design to make it lighter, or bigger? What if you used a plastic bag for the sail? What happens if you attach two lengths of kite string on opposite sides?

Pages 44–45: Can you make a rainbow mobile with rainbow shapes and colours? Or how about a mobile which uses the symbols from weather forecasts?

Page 46: See if you can use the Sun rather than a torch as the light source. You'll need to set up the experiment by a window on a sunny day. You may need to lay a white sheet, or piece of paper, on the floor to catch the rainbow.

Page 47: Can you make a weather station to measure rainfall and wind direction?

- Without the weather to spread the Sun's heat around the world, the central areas of the planet would get hotter and hotter and the poles colder and colder. Nothing would be able to live on Earth.

- Roy Cleveland Sullivan was a park ranger in Shenandoah National Park in Virginia, USA. Between 1942 and 1977, Sullivan was hit by lightning on an incredible seven different occasions and survived all of them. He lost his big toenail in 1942, his eyebrows in 1969 and had his hair set on fire twice.

- To see a rainbow, you must have your back to the Sun. Sometimes double rainbows can form. In the second bow, the colours are always ordered the opposite way round.

- A lightning bolt generates temperatures five times hotter than the 6000°C found at the surface of the Sun.

- Mawsynram is a village in northeastern India. It is the wettest place on Earth, with an average annual rainfall of 11,872 millimetres. Most of it falls during the monsoon season.

- The Atacama Desert in Chile is one of the driest places in the world. To obtain drinking water, Chileans have set up fog catchers that look like giant volleyball nets. The water in sea fog sticks to the nets and is collected.

- The largest types of clouds are known as cumulonimbus clouds, and they contain massive amounts of water. The clouds reach a height of 18 kilometres, which is twice as high as Mount Everest.

- On 6 August 2000, a shower of fish fell in Great Yarmouth, Norfolk, England. Sometimes, strong winds during a thunderstorm can scoop up fish and frogs from rivers or the sea. The animals are carried along in the clouds and later fall as rain!

- At the centre of a tornado, winds can reach up to 600 kilometres per hour, making them the fastest winds on Earth. A tornado leapfrogs across the land causing great damage. It can destroy one house and leave the house next door untouched.

- A tiny drop of water will stay in the Earth's atmosphere for an average of 11 days. If all the water in the air fell at the same time, it could cover the whole of the planet with 25 millimetres of rain.

- The largest hailstone ever recorded fell on 23 July 2010 in Vivian, South Dakota, USA. It measured 20 centimetres in diameter, the size of a tenpin bowling ball!

- The lowest world temperature ever recorded was a bitter −89.6°C at Vostok Station, Antarctica, on 21 July 1983.

- The greatest snowfall recorded was on Mount Rainier, Washington, USA, in 1972, when over 30 metres of snow fell in one winter.

Weather quiz

The answers to these questions can all be found by looking back through the book. See how many you get right. You can check your answers on page 56.

1) How long does it take for the Earth to orbit the Sun?
   A – A day
   B – A month
   C – A year

2) Which layer of Earth's atmosphere is closest to the ground?
   A – Mesosphere
   B – Exosphere
   C – Troposphere

3) Which continent has the coldest climate on Earth?
   A – Asia
   B – Antarctica
   C – Oceania

4) When water is warmed, what does it turn into first?
   A – Vapour
   B – Cloud
   C – Mist

5) What is the centre of a hurricane called?
   A – Ear
   B – Eye
   C – Nose

6) Which of these statements is not true?
   A – Ice weighs less than water
   B – Icebergs float
   C – Only a small part of an iceberg is underwater

7) Where does drought often occur?
   A – In deserts
   B – In the mountains
   C – In jungles

8) How many sides does a snow crystal usually have?
   A – 6
   B – 7
   C – 8

9) Which of these is a current of warm water in the Pacific Ocean?
   A – El Dorado
   B – El Niño
   C – El Greco

10) What happens to seaweed when it is about to rain?
   A – It gets fat
   B – It dries out
   C – It changes colour

11) What is a powerful, spinning wind called?
   A – Tornado
   B – Turbine
   C – Cumulus

12) Lightning is a spark of what?
   A – Ice
   B – Electricity
   C – Gas

Find out more

Books to read

Basher Basics: Weather by Dan Green and Simon Basher, Kingfisher, 2012

Drought (Wild Weather) by Catherine Chambers, Heinemann, 2008

Everything Weather by Kathy Furgang, National Geographic Kids, 2012

Hurricanes and Tornadoes (Wild Weather) by Angela Royston, QED Publishing, 2009

Wild Weather (It's all about..) Kingfisher, 2015

Weather (Eyewitness Project Books), Dorling Kindersley, 2008

Places to visit

The Science Museum, London
www.sciencemuseum.org.uk
The museum's *atmosphere* gallery is an exciting, interactive world with land, oceans and ice above your head. Find out how climate works, what the world's climate is now and what it might be in the future. The gallery also shows you the key instruments and methods used by scientists who study climate change.

Weston Park Museum, Sheffield
www.museums-sheffield.org.uk/museums/ weston-park
At this museum you can find out how weather works, and its effects on the world. An exhibition shows you what life in the Arctic is like. You can even have a go at building your own mini igloo.

National Maritime Museum Cornwall, Falmouth
www.nmmc.co.uk
Interactive exhibits at this museum show you how different weather systems pass over Britain. Find out about the history of weather forecasting and see a weather station in action. You will see how instruments measure the wind, rain, sunlight and much more.

Websites

www.metoffice.gov.uk/education
Here are lots of fun games and activities to help you learn about the weather.

www.dynamicearth.co.uk/kids/ scienceexplored/Weather
This site tells you how hurricanes form and how lightning is made, and you can find out how to make your own weather station.

www.econet.org.uk/weather/whatis.html
These pages have some useful weather information, including a fact list about different types of clouds.

Weather quiz answers

1) C   7) A
2) C   8) A
3) B   9) B
4) A   10) A
5) B   11) A
6) C   12) B